GILES

The Collection 2010

My dear dear (and very best friend) Julia

If and when you feel a bit 'low' here a real
of Giles.

GILES

The Collection 2010

EXPRESS NEWSPAPERS

hamlyn

An Hachette UK Company
www.hachette.co.uk

First published in Great Britain in 2009 by
Hamlyn, a division of Octopus Publishing Group Ltd
2–4 Heron Quays, London E14 4JP
www.octopusbooks.co.uk

Introduction and cartoon selection by Fiona Tucker

ISBN 978-0-600-62046-4

A CIP catalogue record for this book is available from the British Library

Printed in the UK by CPI William Clowes Beccles NR34 7TL

3 5 7 9 10 8 6 4 2

Contents

Introduction

The Giles Annual has been engaging the nation's imagination and humour for over fifty years, and they are as popular with Express readers today as they were when they first began.

Although Giles began his newspaper cartoon career at the much more left-wing Reynold's News in 1937, he is known primarily for his cartoons in the Daily Express and Sunday Express, for whom he worked from 1943 until the end of his career in 1991.

While Giles's politics were not always aligned to those of Express Newspapers, it was nevertheless a very long, successful and prosperous working partnership between the two. During his time with Express, Giles became the highest-earning cartoonist of his time.

The concept of a Giles Annual was first conceived in 1940 (when Giles was still at Reynold's News) in response to a reader's suggestion that an Annual would be the perfect Christmas gift to send to troops serving overseas in the Second World War. The inaugural Annual didn't appear, however, until 1946, when Giles was working for Express Newspapers.

Until his death in 1995, Giles played a major role in the production of the Annuals, selecting all the cartoons himself – a task he found difficult. He felt that the topicality of his cartoons, which appeared on a daily basis, did not translate easily to a yearly publication and he worried that many readers would forget by December an issue that appeared in a cartoon much earlier in the year. Providing explanatory material was mooted but proved too difficult, and many of the more topical cartoons, for which Giles had a particular talent and affection, never made the final cut. But he needn't have worried – the Annuals have been bestsellers since their inception.

The popularity of the Giles Annuals, and of the man himself, remains today, almost fifteen years after his death. While they no longer have the personal input of his genius, the Annuals are, and will continue to be, a testament to one of the great cartoonists and social commentators of our time.

Battle of the Sexes

"And now we come to Lesson Six, gentlemen – how to creep in without waking the wife after a night out with the boys."

Sunday Express, November 28, 1948

"Don't worry, son – when she reads how easy they're going to make it to get a divorce
she'll change her mind and marry you after all."

Sunday Express, April 20, 1952

"You've got to hand it to him – hollering all last week at the T.U.C conference for equal pay for women."

Daily Express, September 15, 1953

"When I said 'For better or worse' yesterday I hadn't seen that hat."

Sunday Express, April 21, 1957

"I don't suppose there are many husbands who spent a wonderful day celebrating Sir Winston's wedding anniversary and forgot it was his own."

Sunday Express, September 14, 1958

"His resolution to get the morning tea lasted well this year – ran right through to the second of January."

Sunday Express, January 3, 1960

"They have a hard life, don't they? We get them up and feed them – secretaries look after them all day – barmaids look after them all evening – now we've got Train Hostesses."

Sunday Express, September 24, 1961

"Don't get up dear, it's Mother's Day – I'll go down and make the tea."

Sunday Express, March 5, 1967

"Can't come out today, boys – thanks to that fool of an M.P. calling women 'inferior and second-class citizens'."

Sunday Express, January 30, 1972

"There's certainly no discrimination between the sexes in this house. I let the women graduate from menial kitchen duties to concrete mixing and so forth."

Sunday Express, February 4, 1973

"Mummy says as you forgot to take her breakfast up for Mother's Day she forgot to get up and get your lunch."

Sunday Express, April 1, 1973

"You read that the secretarial agencies are calling for grannies and older women?
Well your wife has engaged one for you in my place."

Daily Express, May 15, 1973

"You'll like your new secretary, sir, supplied under the new no-sex-discrimination Act."

Daily Express, December 11, 1975

"That takes care of the last two weeks – what happened to the last 14 years?"

Daily Express, July 13, 1976

"Henery! Stop committing adultery at once!"

Daily Express, September 23, 1976

"My automatic washing-up machine never breaks down – he wouldn't dare!"

Daily Express, February 11, 1977

"I move that under the Sex Discrimination Rules we have a new one to let the MEN have five minutes start."

Daily Express, February 21, 1977

"Pardon my mirth, Romeo."

Daily Express, September 30, 1977

"Don't believe everything you read in the papers, Travolta."

Daily Express, December 12, 1978

"I'd go straight home if I were you, sir – your wife's fitted a Spy-in-the-cab."

Daily Express, March 8, 1979

"'Fetch this, get that, my man' – ever since she's had a woman Prime Minister."

Sunday Express, May 6, 1979

"I don't think Dad's eight miles to work by bike is saving as much petrol as Mum thinks."

Daily Express, June 28, 1979

"Her husband knows exactly what he wants – whatever she says he's going to get."

Daily Express, August 14, 1979

"Yes, I remember well this is where we first discussed the age of consent, you also discussed it with Florrie Finch, Queenie Quinn, and most of the other WAAF's in my outfit."

Sunday Express, September 16, 1979

"Forty quids' worth of roses because HE thinks SHE sent him a Valentine's card... actually, I sent it."

Daily Express, February 14, 1985

"Never mind where I come in the Anne Diamond ratings of mixed-up Macho males –
get my tea, woman."

Daily Express, September 18, 1986

"Mrs Thatcher didn't like being called only a housewife. Nor did my wife."

Daily Express, July 2, 1987

"Now we come to the bit where Father's come out without any money and Mother pays."

Sunday Express, March 13, 1988

"If the experts are right your daughter's marriage has a good chance of survival."

Daily Express, May 10, 1988

The Joy of Children

"Bright idea of yours – taking them to the circus – wasn't it?"

Sunday Express, December 29, 1946

"When I say 'Class, remove smog masks,' I wonder how many little mouths we shall find full of nasty, sticky little sweets?"

Daily Express, October 29, 1953

"DON'T let 'em off in the street, DON'T put 'em in Auntie Vera's bed, DON'T put 'em in baby's pram, DON'T tie 'em on the cat – and they call it a free country!"

Daily Express, November 5, 1954

"Grandma can't find her Sunday dress – what was the Guy Fawkes you burnt on Friday wearing at the time?"

Sunday Express, November 7, 1954

"Not only are these milk tablets issued to schools highly beneficial, but most children prefer them." (OFFICIAL)

Daily Express, March 8, 1955

"If they put a boy on TV just for swallowing a few nails think what a hero you'll be when they find you're full of hammers."

Daily Express, November 1, 1960

"Winston Churchill's doctor lets <u>him</u> smoke cigars while he's poorly."

Daily Express, November 22, 1960

"Assuming their teachers do go on strike and we've got to have them at home a few more weeks..."

Sunday Express, April 9, 1961

"After reprimanding him for whacking my knee with his conker, accused then threatened to exercise his powers under the new Bill and sue the Chief Constable."

Sunday Express, November 7, 1963

"Mother's very cross with you all for hanging baby out of the window on a wire to see if he can walk in space."

Sunday Express, March 21, 1965

"And this comment from your music teacher – 'I hope your boy enjoys his holiday as much as I'm going to enjoy mine'..."

Sunday Express, July 21, 1968

"That's right – you DID hear me tell them to go and get lost for four days up a mountain."

Daily Express, April 26, 1973

"Yes, I read that black is fashionable, black is provocative. Upstairs, first door on the right – BATHROOM!"

Daily Express, June 24, 1977

"Methinks you are about to receive a standing ovation from Chalky."

Daily Express, October 14, 1977

"That wasn't an unidentified flying object – we saw you!"

Daily Express, February 22, 1978

"St. George to Dragon – I give you ten seconds to get off my new flower bed – over and out."

Sunday Express, April 23, 1978

"We didn't have enough money for an ice cream, but the nice man let us trade in the car."

Sunday Express, June 4, 1978

"Hold it right there! Will the brighter pupil inform the less-bright pupils of an antidote to his latest concoction?"

Daily Express, September 28, 1978

"We've been tobogganing – Dad's in Ward 10 but the sledge is all right."

Sunday Express, December 3, 1978

"That one will go far – booked the Chief Constable for lingering with intent outside police HQ."

Daily Express, April 3, 1979

"They gave the Queen a small bouquet for it."

Daily Express, May 31, 1979

"Methinks those who are not putting in their reports hath already sold them to the Sunday papers."

Daily Express, October 9, 1979

"That Head started something sending them home for having short hair – bald as a snooker ball every one of 'em!"

Sunday Express, October 28, 1979

"Introducing Super Glue for the paper chains shows a marked failure to understand the imaginative workings of the modern child's mind, Miss Winslow."

Daily Express, December 13, 1979

"Just two more days of the Year of the Child then the Year of the Adult takes over in this house."

Sunday Express, December 30, 1979

"Poor Penelope – she thought they were going back THIS Tuesday."

Daily Express, September 1, 1981

"Morning, Froid – we hear you're the only boy who did his homework instead of watching football last night."

Daily Express, November 19, 1981

"Whether we can afford the new Star Wars video depends on how much we can get for him on the baby market."

Daily Express, September 25, 1984

"I know Prince Philip and Princess Anne use words like that, but you're not sending this!"

Daily Express, April 10, 1986

Brits on Holiday

"I want to go home."

Daily Express, June 12, 1948

"A pot of tea for three, please."

Daily Express, July 13, 1948

The strange desire of the British to paddle at least once a year.

Daily Express, August 21, 1951

"Very well – let's hear YOU explain in YOUR impeccable Spanish that we've promised Grandma we'll be back in time for the Coronation."

Sunday Express, May 31, 1953

"My wife's got a theory that it doesn't pay to let them know you're English."

Daily Express, June 24, 1953

"The sooner this family learns that NO ENTRADA on a door in Spain means NO ENTRY the better."

Daily Express, June 25, 1953

"Stand by for an acute attack of Grandma's deafness – I'm just going to tell her to get ready for home."

Daily Express, September 14, 1954

"Your wee bairns were collecting them as souvenirs to take home and you didn't know it – a likely story!"

Daily Express, September 17, 1954

"Come, Bertie – 'tis time we were leaving for home."

Sunday Express, January 23, 1955

"All right – space-men have landed and captured Grandma and Auntie Vera. Now go and play something that doesn't make quite so much noise."

Daily Express, August 3, 1955

The Giles Family on holiday. First day.

Daily Express, August 8, 1955

"I got the bus – it's a damn sight quicker."

Daily Express, August 9, 1955

"Good job we left the children at home, or Father would be blaming them because he hasn't caught anything."

Daily Express, August 10, 1955

"Dear Maud, we are staying at a very nice hotel right on the sea front. The weather is lovely and it is such a change to get away from the house for a few days..."

Sunday Express, March 29, 1959

"An enterprising one is our Rhamjah!"

Daily Express, January 24, 1961

"As a matter of fact we do not think this is better than taking one of those chancy holidays in the Med."

Sunday Express, July 28, 1974

"I'll tell you what I think about Bank Holidays by the sea."

Daily Express, May 27, 1975

"Ole! First one down gets the breakfast egg!"

Daily Express, July 22, 1975

"I know I booked a two-week Round-Britain-Tour – but I didn't say anything about me going."

Sunday Express, July 27, 1975

"You didn't phone and cancel our Spanish holiday as a protest against Franco –
you cancelled it because you damn well didn't want to go."

Sunday Express, October 5, 1975

"There goes your mother – off to buy another 20 per cent worth of junk."

Daily Express, July 13, 1977

"Pity our flight was cancelled...Costa del Caballeria will never know what they missed."

Daily Express, August 26, 1977

"The Senora says as the rest of your party couldn't get here, there's a small charge for using their sun."

Daily Express, August 29, 1977

"Mind you, Daddy's on a sticky wicket having to argue about Euro-Elections in English."

Sunday Express, June 3, 1979

"I knew damn well we shouldn't have asked that Aussie taxi driver for the shortest cut to the practice pitch."

Daily Express, November 8, 1979

"Don't forget – we've been staying with Aunty Pru in Blackpool, not with the crooks on the Costa del Sol."

Daily Express, July 5, 1984

"We've got a complaint – they've been in Corfu for three-quarters of an hour and haven't been propositioned."

Daily Express, August 7, 1984

"Explain to Senora that we have come here to escape from the British in Germany."

Daily Express, June 16, 1988

"She says – how she know we not English tourists in disguise?"

Daily Express, July 5, 1988

Protests & Strikes

"This go-slow strike'll shake the people who thought British railways couldn't go any slower."

Sunday Express, November 24, 1946

"You and your flipping rail strike – lost me me newspaper round – that's what you've done."

Sunday Express, May 23, 1954

"Git dahn, some of yer! Git dahn!"

Daily Express, April 21, 1955

"Giving me a cup with no handle and saying 'I hope it chokes you, you blacklegging old scab' ain't forgiving and forgetting, Miss."

Daily Express, August 14, 1956

"I think it's a protest march of the boys from your class, Mr. Chalk."

Daily Express, April 10, 1958

"We've just been de-bagged by de-Teddyfied Teddy Boys."

Sunday Express, October 12, 1958

"Skip this one."

Sunday Express, September 20, 1959

"At least it's put some life in the blessed game."

Sunday Express, April 10, 1960

"You can come out, Oswald – it was only one of those rotters bursting a paper bag."

Daily Express, April 4, 1961

"While you've been having your protest march most of them have slipped out for an emergency meeting in the Pig & Flute."

Daily Express, March 13, 1962

"Another Communist inspired wildcat strike."

Sunday Express, February 17, 1963

"Can his Grandma have 6-4 the Rail Strike's on, 100-1 the Dock Strike's off, 60-1 the Banks Strike's on, 100-1 the School Strike's off, 6-4 the BOAC Pilots..."

Daily Express, November 30, 1967

'Damn!'

Daily Express, April 2, 1968

"Closing our local while we're on strike is not the kind of support we're looking for, laddie."

Sunday Express, July 26, 1970

"I see they did not think much of your offer to take their minds off
the national crisis by doing your bird and animal imitations."

Daily Express, February 27, 1973

"In the meantime I'm prepared to put up with me sunken bath. Boy! another bucket of asses milk."

Daily Express, March 13, 1973

"'Come in, Quasimodo' doesn't help, Vicar."

Daily Express, February 2, 1977

"This sort of thing could get the LSE a bad name."

Daily Express, February 26, 1977

"Blooming cheek! We all bought you a drink only last week to celebrate *your* pay increase!"

Daily Express, October 31, 1977

"They're lovely duckies – unfortunately I'm what you might call a 'blackleg'".

Sunday Express, October 1, 1978

"Blacklegging, I think they call it in industrial circles, Farquharson."

Sunday Express, April 1, 1979

"Just in case we find 500 coppers lined up at each end of Downing Street."

Daily Express, May 29, 1980

"You can stop coming to work in disguise, Doctor, we have decided on non-belligerent action."

Sunday Express, June 8, 1980

"Greenham and NGA pickets are enough for one week without bloody Cabbage Patch dolls."

Daily Express, December 1, 1983

"Here comes our instant strike-breaker."

Daily Express, May 1, 1984

"We're only wearing them to help that lot over there with their inquiries."

Daily Express, August 20, 1985

"You bet I'm shouting! Everyone's making as many calls as they can before the BT strike begins!"

Sunday Express, January 25, 1987

"A gentleman from the postmen's union is waiting for you in the front room."

Daily Express, November 19, 1987

"If my regular battleaxe wasn't gallivanting about on strike she'd have had this lot out of here sharp on the dot."

Daily Express, February 4, 1988

'Tis the Season

"Let's buy Grandma something really useful – like a train-set or some roller skates."

Daily Express, December 12, 1950

"I heard Dad tell Mr. Smith that he's going to buy Mum a lovely set of new tyres for the car for Christmas."

Daily Express, December 22, 1953

"If Modom doesn't soon make her mind up, Modom is going to get a
Yuletide ding across the back of the ear."

Daily Express, December 21, 1954

"His insurance claim will look good – 'DESCRIPTION OF VEHICLE ... Stage coach.
PASSENGER'S OCCUPATION ... Father Christmas'."

Daily Express, November 22, 1955

"Come and say 'Good Morning' to what you called 'The sweetest Christmas present you have had'."

Daily Express, December 27, 1956

"Remember the big laugh because I got Casualty Ward for Christmas?
Well, I've made forty-two pounds fourteen and six in Christmas pud. sixpences."

Sunday Express, December 27, 1959

"Fellers, you know that hamster we've bought Grandma for Christmas...?"

Daily Express, December 10, 1960

"Here they come – look happy."

Daily Express, December 20, 1960

"They can put me in orbit anytime. They can put me anywhere they like except that Merry Christmas store where we work."

Sunday Express, December 3, 1961

"If he ad-libs once more and says 'How goes it with the Three Wise Guys?' something's going to happen to that wire."

Sunday Express, December 17, 1961

"Pity if he heard you refer to him as a dreary misconception of an obsolete legend – that's the general manager."

Daily Express, December 19, 1961

"Morning, Sir – remember going home before Christmas in a funny little hat and kissing me under the mistletoe?"

Daily Express, December 27, 1961

"Now this merry festive death-ray gun, Madam, lets out a stream of devastating nerve gas which disintegrates any living object within range. And boy, do I wish it did!"

Daily Express, December 17, 1970

"Wife-swopping is the rave this year – Gentleman wants to know
if we'll swop his for a colour TV."

Daily Express, December 14, 1971

"I've written and told the Express the only way they can solve my
Christmas present problem is by sending me a cheque."

Daily Express, December 4, 1975

"I'll toss you for who reminds him he's playing Father Christmas at the office party tonight."

Daily Express, December 23, 1975

"Three shop-lifting, two drunk and disorderly."

Daily Express, December 12, 1977

"Repeat again, everybody: 'Mother does not want any new puppies, budgies, pussies, or bunnies for Christmas'."

Daily Express, December 16, 1977

"Good morning, Dad. The aunts say as you've got ten days off for Christmas they can stay another week."

Daily Express, December 28, 1978

"Hold it, man – we can't go around punching happy shoppers just because they poked their Christmas tree in your eye."

Daily Express, December 11, 1979

"I don't think Auntie Esther meant her present to be worn OVER your topcoat, Dad."

Daily Express, December 27, 1979

"Grandma's been a great help. She's packed all the presents but forgot to label which one's which."

Sunday Express, December 18, 1983

"Well that should put paid to the legend of Father Christmas."

Daily Express, December 24, 1984

"Last year the little dears did him up in his Christmas cave – this year he's going to be ready for them."

Sunday Express, December 1, 1985

"Those Teddy bears you 'found' up here and put in the Christie's sale were the twins' Christmas presents."

Sunday Express, December 15, 1985

"Hold tight, Dad – someone's just found a pre-Christmas sale ticket on that bed jacket you gave her."

Sunday Express, December 28, 1986

"'Noel' louder, please Miss – while they remove Father Christmas for shop-lifting."

Daily Express, December 15, 1987

"Dad says the Germans have got it right banning Forces Christmas parties in Germany –
he says he's for banning Christmas parties everywhere."

Daily Express, December 20, 1988

"Wakey, wakey – the lady's little boys can't get their Garfield and Odie suits off."

Daily Express, January 3, 1989

"The new rule – we all bow out of the room walking backwards since he's been made a King in the Christmas play."

Sunday Express, December 10, 1989